D0058708

꧁ Presented to ꧂

Althea

꧁ On the occasion of ꧂

With prayers and best wishes
from

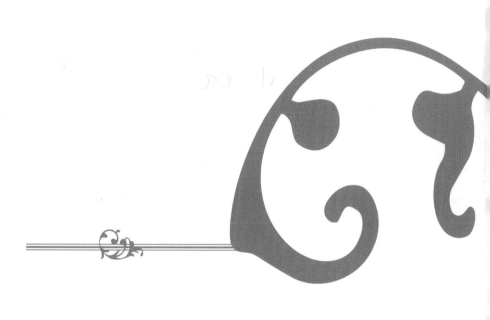

My First Book of
SAINTS

Written by
Kathleen M. Muldoon
& Susan Helen Wallace, FSP

Illustrated by
Tom Kinarney
& Patricia R. Mattozzi

Pauline
BOOKS & MEDIA
Boston

Library of Congress Cataloging-in-Publication Data

Muldoon, Kathleen M.
My first book of saints / written by Kathleen M. Muldoon and Susan
Helen Wallace ; illustrated by Tom Kinarney and Patricia R. Mattozzi.
p. cm.
ISBN-13: 978-0-8198-4917-5
ISBN-10: 0-8198-4917-0
1. Christian saints--Biography--Juvenile literature. I. Wallace, Susan
Helen, 1940- II. Kinarney, Tom, ill. III. Mattozzi, Patricia R. ill. IV.
Title.
BX4658.M754 2012
270.092'2--dc23

2012027383

Cover design by Mary Joseph Peterson, FSP

Illustrated by Tom Kinarney and Patricia R. Mattozzi

All rights reserved. No part of this book may be reproduced or
transmitted in any form or by any means, electronic or mechanical,
including photocopying, recording, or by any information storage and
retrieval system, without permission in writing from the publisher.

"P" and PAULINE are registered trademarks of the Daughters of St.
Paul.

Copyright © 2006, Kathleen M. Muldoon

Published by Pauline Books & Media, 50 Saint Pauls Avenue, Boston,
MA 02130-3491

Printed in Korea

MFBS SIPSKOGUNKYO4-24031 4917-0

www.pauline.org

Pauline Books & Media is the publishing house of the Daughters of St.
Paul, an international congregation of women religious serving the
Church with the communications media.

2 3 4 5 6 7 8 9   18 17 16 15 14

Contents

Blessed Mother, Mary

When Mary was a teenager, an angel brought her a message from God. God wanted her to be the mother of his son, Jesus. God had picked Mary from all the women on Earth! Mary was probably scared. But she trusted God. She told the angel "yes."

After Jesus was born, Mary and her husband, Joseph, raised him. Mary was with Jesus when he died on the cross. Now she is in heaven. She is our Blessed Mother. She loves us and prays for us.

Mary always said "yes" to God. She will help us to obey.

Mary lived during the first century A.D.

She was born in Palestine.

We celebrate her birthday on September 8.

We celebrate her feast day as the Mother of God on January 1.

Saint Peter the Apostle

Peter was a hardworking fisherman in Galilee. He had a family and a boat. One day, his brother, Andrew, brought him to meet Jesus. Peter and Andrew became part of Jesus's first group of apostles. Peter loved Jesus very much, and Jesus loved and trusted Peter. Before Jesus's crucifixion, Peter denied knowing Jesus. Afterward, he was ashamed and sorry. Jesus forgave him. In fact, Jesus made Peter the leader of his Church—the first pope. Peter died a brave martyr for Jesus and became a great saint.

Saint Peter, please teach me to trust Jesus totally.

Saint Peter lived at the time of Jesus and died around the year 67.

He lived in Galilee.

We celebrate two feast days: one on June 29 with Saint Paul, the other on February 22.

Saints Anne and Joachim

Joachim and Anne lived a long time ago. They were married to each other. They prayed that someone would come to save their Jewish people. God heard their prayers. He sent them a beautiful daughter. They named her Mary. She was loving and good. One day the Angel Gabriel told Mary that God wanted her to become the mother of Jesus, his Son. Mary said yes! She married Joseph, a gentle carpenter. Joachim and Anne became the grandparents of Jesus, our Savior.

Saint Anne and Saint Joachim, please help me to love Mary and Jesus as you did.

Saint Anne and Saint Joachim lived in the first century A.D.

They were born in Palestine.

We celebrate their feast day on July 26.

Saint Joseph

God chose Joseph to be Jesus's father on earth. The Bible tells us that Joseph was an honest man. He was a good husband and father. He found a safe place for Jesus to be born.

Saint Joseph lived during the first century A.D.

He was born in Palestine.

We celebrate his feast day as the husband of Mary on March 19.

Joseph worked very hard to take care of Jesus and Mary. He was a carpenter. He did not have powerful tools like the ones we have today. He used simple tools. He built different things like chairs and tables.

From heaven, Saint Joseph watches over all fathers. We can ask him to keep us close to Jesus and Mary. We can ask him to help us with our work.

Saint Elizabeth of Hungary

Elizabeth was a princess. She married Ludwig, who was a king. They had three children. One winter, Ludwig died. His relatives sent Elizabeth and her children away from the castle. Some Franciscan brothers helped them. Elizabeth's family helped them, too. After that, Elizabeth understood what it was like to be poor. Soon Elizabeth wanted to help others who were poor. She built a hospital. She started a shelter. She cooked meals for homeless people. Elizabeth worked hard to make the world a better place.

Saint Elizabeth, please help me to be cheerful in good times and in bad.

Saint Elizabeth lived from 1207–1231.

She was born in Hungary.

We celebrate her feast day on November 17.

Saint Benedict

Young Benedict wanted to grow close to God. He went into the hills to live alone in a quiet cave. A holy monk showed Benedict how to live as a hermit. The young man listened, prayed, and worked hard. He learned to grow his own food. Other men in the area heard about Benedict and wanted to follow him. Together they built a monastery. Soon there were twelve communities of monks leading lives of prayer, work, and charity. Today Saint Benedict's many followers are known as Benedictines.

Saint Benedict lived from 480–547.

He lived in Italy.

We celebrate his feast day on July 11.

Saint Benedict, please teach me to pray and work as you did.

Saint Thérèse
of Lisieux

When Thérèse was a young girl, she was so sick she nearly died. She asked Mary to make her well. Then something special happened. Mary's statue smiled at Thérèse. After that, Thérèse was cured!

Thérèse became a nun when she was fifteen. She was kind and loving to everyone. She prayed for everyone. She did the jobs that no one else wanted to do. Thérèse never did anything great or special, but she did *everything* with love. This was her "little way" of coming closer to God.

Saint Thérèse will show us many little ways to love God and one another.

Saint Thérèse lived from 1873–1897.

She was born in France.

We celebrate her feast day on October 1.

Saint Damien of Molokai

Joseph got in lots of trouble when he was young. But when he grew up, he changed. He became a priest known as Father Damien. He went to Hawaii and worked hard to spread the love of Jesus. He heard about some people who were very sick with leprosy. They lived on an island called Molokai. Father Damien took care of them. He built houses and brought in clean water. After fifteen years, he caught leprosy too. Father Damien helped over a thousand sick people on Molokai.

Saint Damien lived from 1840–1889.

He was born in Belgium.

We celebrate his feast day on May 10.

Saint Damien, please show me how to be helpful to my family and friends.

Saint Kateri Tekakwitha

Kateri was an American Indian. Her mother was a Christian Algonquin. Her father was a Mohawk chief. When she was young, her mother died. Kateri lived with her aunt and uncle. When she was twenty, missionaries came to her village. She learned about Jesus and was baptized. People in the village were angry with Kateri. They didn't want her to be Christian. The missionaries helped her escape to a Christian village. There she lived a happy life. Saint Kateri is known as the Lily of the Mohawks.

Saint Kateri, please teach me how to be faithful to Jesus as you were.

Saint Kateri lived from 1656–1680.

She lived in what are now the United States and Canada.

We celebrate her feast on July 14 (United States) or April 17 (Canada).

Saint Paul

Paul obeyed all the laws of the Jewish religion. But at first he was angry at people who believed in Jesus. Once, Paul was going to arrest some of them. He saw a bright light. He heard the voice of Jesus. Then he knew that Jesus is the Son of God!

Paul began teaching everyone about Jesus. That made some people hate him. But Paul was brave. He traveled everywhere. He wrote letters. He was even put to death because he would not stop talking and teaching about Jesus.

Saint Paul lived from about the years 5–67.

He was born in Cilicia (now part of the country of Turkey).

We celebrate his feast day on June 29.

We celebrate his becoming a Christian on January 25.

We can pray to Saint Paul to help us love Jesus with our whole heart.

Blessed Teresa of Calcutta

Mother Teresa worried about the many poor people in India. She knew Jesus wanted her to help those who were without hope. Thousands in Calcutta were sick and dying. Mother Teresa and the Missionaries of Charity started homes to care for them. Some got better. Others died peacefully. Soon the sisters started helping in other countries, too. They fed the hungry. They took care of the sick. Mother Teresa and her sisters wanted to weave a chain of love around the world.

Blessed Teresa, teach me to care about people who need help.

Blessed Teresa lived from 1910–1997.

She was born in Macedonia, formerly Albania.

We celebrate her feast day on September 5.

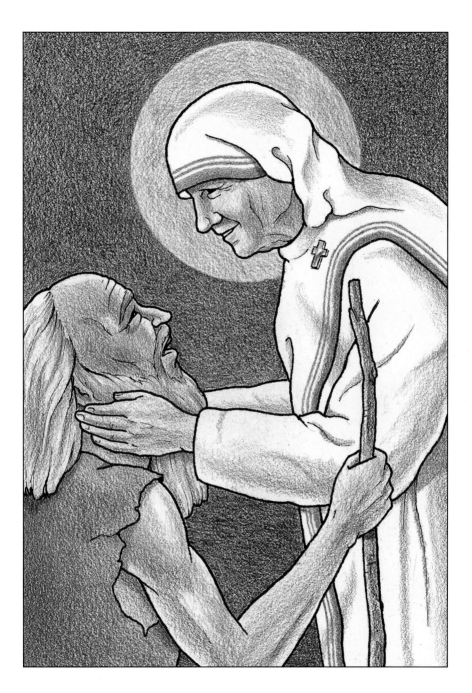

Saint Francis Xavier

Francis was from a wealthy family. When he grew up, he went to study in Paris. There he met Ignatius of Loyola. Soon Ignatius became a priest. He started the Society of Jesus, also called the Jesuits. Francis became a Jesuit priest too. Father Francis traveled to many foreign lands. He preached to large crowds of people. Thousands asked to be baptized. Francis was so happy! He had many exciting adventures. Then Father Francis became sick. He was on his way to preach in China when he died.

Saint Francis, help me to show my love for Jesus by helping others.

Saint Francis lived from 1506–1552.

He was born in Spain.

We celebrate his feast day on December 3.

Saint Bernadette Soubirous

Bernadette's family was poor, and Bernadette was often sick. When she was fourteen, she saw the Blessed Mother in a cave. Bernadette told her parents and her priest. They did not believe her.

Saint Bernadette lived from 1844–1879.

She was born in France.

We celebrate her feast day on April 16.

Mary kept visiting Bernadette. She talked to her. She asked Bernadette to pray for sinners. One day, the Blessed Mother told Bernadette to dig in the ground. Water came out. It healed many people. Then people began to believe Bernadette!

We can ask Saint Bernadette to help us know and love the Blessed Mother and to do what is right no matter what others think.

Saint Dominic Savio

Dominic was a blacksmith's son. He had a big dream. He wanted to become a priest. He had lots of friends at school and always studied hard. Often he visited the chapel to pray to his "best friend," Jesus. Dominic wanted to be like his school principal, Father John Bosco. When Dominic was fourteen, he became very ill. He went home to recover, but he didn't get better. Soon after he went home, he died. Now both Dominic and Father Bosco have been named saints.

Saint Dominic Savio, patron saint of young people, help me to stay close to Jesus, too.

Saint Dominic lived from 1842–1857.

He was born in Italy.

We celebrate his feast day on March 9.

Saint Katharine Drexel

Katharine lived in Philadelphia. Her father was a very wealthy man. Katharine, her sisters, and her mother gave food and clothing to needy people. Katharine decided to become a nun. She started a new religious order. It's called the Sisters of the Blessed Sacrament. The sisters wanted to teach Native American and African-American children.

Saint Katharine lived from 1858–1955.

She was born in the United States.

We celebrate her feast day on March 3.

Mother Katharine inherited her father's money. With it she opened schools in different cities, helping many children.

Saint Katharine, please help me to be as loving and unselfish as you were.

Saint Francis of Assisi

When he was young, Francis wore fancy clothes. He had many nice things. But he *really* wanted to be a knight. So Francis went off to war. Then he had a dream about how Jesus wanted him to live.

Francis gave up his riches. He started helping the poor. Men and women joined him. They wanted to live more like Jesus. They wanted to serve the poor, too.

Saint Francis lived from 1181–1226.

He was born in Italy.

We celebrate his feast day on October 4.

Francis had a special love for every living thing, even tiny ants! We can ask Saint Francis to help us care for one another and for all God's creatures.

Saint Clare of Assisi

Clare and Brother Francis lived in the same city. Clare noticed that Francis spent his life for God. He took care of the poor. Other young men followed him and became friars, too. Clare was the first woman to follow Francis. She and her sister, Agnes, started the order now known as Poor Clares. When Clare was ill, she couldn't go to chapel for Christmas Mass. Miraculously, she saw the Mass in her room! That's why she's the patron saint of television. Now Clare, Francis, and Agnes are all saints.

Saint Clare, please help me to see and imitate the good in others.

Saint Clare lived from 1193–1253.

She lived her whole life in Assisi, Italy.

We celebrate her feast day on August 11.

Blessed Charles de Foucauld

Charles was a French soldier who had turned away from God. When he was twenty-eight, he rediscovered his faith. He traveled to the Middle East and became a monk. Later he was ordained a priest. He went to live in the Sahara desert in Algeria. There he lived as a hermit, loving God and serving others. He offered weary travelers food and rest. He prayed with them. Father Charles became a kind, holy friend to every person he met. He tried to treat everyone just as Jesus would treat them.

Blessed Charles lived from 1858–1916.

He was born in France.

We celebrate his feast day on December 1.

Blessed Charles, please teach me to treat everyone kindly.

Saint Michael the Archangel

Angels are holy spirits. They are God's special messengers. Saint Michael is an angel called an *archangel.* Archangels are angel leaders. Michael is head of all the angels in heaven.

Saint Michael has lived since the creation of the world.

We celebrate his feast day on September 29.

A long time ago there was a battle in heaven. Good angels fought bad angels. Saint Michael led the good angels. They won the war against Lucifer, who was the leader of the bad angels.

Today police and soldiers pray to Saint Michael to help them defend what is right and good.

We should always try to do what is right. Saint Michael will help us!

Saint Rose of Lima

Baby Isabel reminded her family of a beautiful flower. That's why they called her Rose. Rose often spoke to God in prayer. She was kind and helped many poor people. To earn money, she grew vegetables. Then she sold them in the market. She also did fine sewing work. Rose became a third order Dominican nun. She lived in a hut in her parents' backyard. There she worked hard, prayed, and shared her joy with others. Rose's face was lovely, but her heart was even lovelier.

Saint Rose, please teach me to be kind to others every day.

Saint Rose lived from 1586–1617.

She was born in Peru.

We celebrate her feast day on August 23.

Saint Thomas More

Thomas was a husband and father in London. He loved his family and his Catholic faith. He was a fair, honest lawyer who served King Henry VIII. Thomas prayed every day and helped the poor as often as possible. One day, King Henry decided to become the head of a new church. He wanted the Church of England to be apart from the Catholic Church. Thomas would not agree to this. He was loyal to his king, but his first loyalty was to God. Thomas was executed for his faith.

Saint Thomas More lived from 1478–1535.

He was born in England.

We celebrate his feast day on June 22.

Saint Thomas, please teach me to stand up for what I believe in.

Saint Faustina Kowalska

Helena only went to school for three years. First she worked as a maid. Then she became a nun. Her new name was Sister Faustina. Sometimes Jesus let Sister Faustina see him. Jesus asked her to tell people how much he loved them. Jesus said that he wanted everyone to trust him.

Saint Faustina lived from 1905–1938.

She was born in Poland.

We celebrate her feast day on October 5.

Saint Faustina wrote a book about what Jesus told her. An artist painted a picture of Jesus. It showed how Jesus looked when Faustina saw him. This picture shows us how loving, kind, and forgiving Jesus is to us!

Saint Faustina will help us to trust always in Jesus.

Saint André Bessette

André was a brother in the Congregation of the Holy Cross. He became the doorkeeper at their college.

Saint André lived from 1845–1937.

He was born in Canada.

We celebrate his feast day on January 6.

André never forgot a dream he once had. He saw a big church. What could it mean? He prayed to Jesus and Saint Joseph. They helped him to understand that he should build that church. Many people asked Brother André to pray for them. Miraculous healings kept happening. Now there is a beautiful church in Montréal. We know it as Saint Joseph's Oratory.

Saint André, help me to love and honor Saint Joseph as you did.

Blesseds Jacinta and Francisco Marto

Francisco, his sister Jacinta, and their cousin Lucia cared for their sheep near the town of Fatima. The Blessed Mother appeared to them six times. She told them they would someday go to heaven. There was a terrible war in Europe. Mary asked them to pray the Rosary every day for peace. Doing as Mary asked made them very happy. Jacinta and Francisco both died only a few years later.

Blessed Jacinta lived from 1910–1920.

Blessed Francisco lived from 1908–1919.

They were born in Portugal.

We celebrate their feast day on February 20.

Blessed Jacinta and Blessed Francisco, please teach me to pray for peace as you did.

Saint Anthony

Fernando's parents taught him to love God. Fernando also liked to study. He remembered everything he read. Fernando became a priest when he was a young man. He was called Father Anthony. Father Anthony did not tell anyone how smart he was.

Saint Anthony lived from 1195–1231.

He was born in Portugal.

We celebrate his feast day on June 13.

One day, the other priests needed someone to teach. Only Anthony could do it. Everyone was surprised to see how much he knew! Father Anthony loved Jesus very much. He wanted everyone to love Jesus too. This is why he became a great teacher in the Church.

Saint Anthony will help us when we need to learn and remember things.

Saint Marie of the Incarnation Guyard

Marie Guyard was a French widow. "God is calling me to be an Ursuline sister," she told her family. After several years, the Blessed Mother appeared to her. "I want you to build a convent in a new land," Mary said. Marie traveled to Québec, Canada. She and her sisters learned the native languages of the people of the First Nations. They opened a convent where the sisters taught the children and lovingly cared for the sick. Mother Marie lived in her new country for the rest of her life.

Saint Marie lived from 1599–1672.

She was born in France.

We celebrate her feast day on April 30.

Saint Marie, teach me to be loving and generous in the service of others.

Saint Lorenzo Ruiz

Young Lorenzo loved Jesus. He was an altar server. When he grew up, he was falsely accused of a serious crime. His missionary friends helped him to escape danger. He sailed with them to Japan, but Christian missionaries weren't wanted there. Officials tried to force them to give up their belief in Jesus. With his rosary in his hands, Lorenzo said, "If I had a thousand lives to give, I would offer them all for Jesus." He died bravely and became the first martyr and saint of the Philippines.

Saint Lorenzo, please show me how to be brave and holy.

Saint Lorenzo lived from 1600–1637.

He was born in the Philippines.

We celebrate his feast day on September 28.

Saint Bakhita

When Bakhita was nine, some bad men kidnapped her. They sold her as a slave. The slave owners were harsh to her. But Bakhita never hated them. She stayed gentle and kind.

Saint Bakhita lived from 1869–1947.

She was born in Sudan.

We celebrate her feast day on February 8.

Finally, a man from Italy helped her. He knew that people should not be slaves. He brought Bakhita to Italy. After she became free, Bakhita joined the Catholic Church. She loved Jesus so much that she chose to be a nun. For the rest of her life she cared for poor and sick people. She was so gentle that everyone called her their "Mother."

We can ask Saint Bakhita to make us gentle and kind, too.

Saint John Neumann

John studied hard. There were so many priests in Bohemia, though. John heard that the United States needed priests. He left his home and traveled to New York. There he became a priest. The people welcomed him. At first he lived in a log cabin. Even the church was built of logs! Finally Father Neumann became bishop of Philadelphia. He opened Catholic schools and built many churches. He spoke twelve languages. Father Neumann worked very hard. He wanted to make life better for all his people.

Saint John Neumann, teach me to spread Jesus's love just as you did.

Saint John lived from 1811–1860.

He was born in Bohemia, now the Czech Republic.

We celebrate his feast day on January 5.

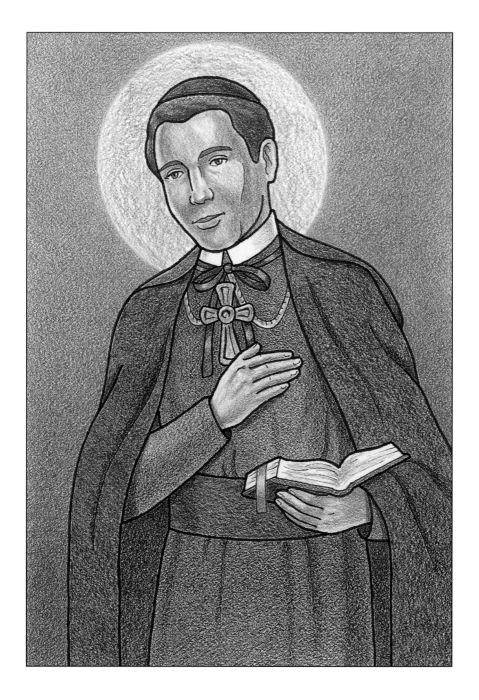

Saint Teresa of Avila

Teresa was pretty and happy. She loved to pray. Then she grew to be a teenager. Suddenly she wasn't so interested in praying anymore! After a few years, though, Teresa began to think more about Jesus and how much she loved him. She decided to become a Carmelite nun. Jesus often spoke to her in her heart. He asked her to start new convents. He also asked her to help other nuns and priests to follow his teachings. Teresa was a great leader. She was always faithful to Jesus and to his Church.

Saint Teresa, please help me to remember to pray often.

Saint Teresa lived from 1515–1582.

She was born in Spain.

We celebrate her feast day on October 15.

Saint Juan Diego

Juan Diego was a poor farmer. Every morning he walked fifteen miles to go to Mass. One day he saw the Blessed Mother on a hill. "Ask the bishop to build a church here," Mary said.

But the bishop did not believe Juan. So the Blessed Mother put her picture on Juan Diego's cape. Then the bishop believed and built the church.

Juan Diego had told the Blessed Mother, "Please send somebody important to see the bishop. I am nobody." But God showed him that he was somebody.

Saint Juan Diego will show us that God's love makes us all special.

Saint Juan Diego lived from 1474–1548.

He was born in Mexico.

We celebrate his feast day on December 9.

Saint Gianna Molla

Doctor Gianna Molla and her husband, Pietro, had three children. Gianna was so happy. She was expecting a new baby. Her doctors found she had cancer. Gianna wanted the doctors to help her. She didn't want anything to harm her unborn baby, though. She had an operation. It was a success! Gianna's healthy baby girl was born safely. But a week later, Gianna became very ill and died. When her daughter Gianna Emanuela grew up, she became a doctor, just like her beloved mother.

Saint Gianna, please help me to be as loving and brave as you were.

Saint Gianna lived from 1922–1962.

She was born in Italy.

We celebrate her feast day on April 28.

Saint Sharbel Makhluf

Joseph Makhluf cared for his family's sheep. He often prayed and thought about God. When he was twenty-three, he joined the monastery of Saint Maron. He chose to be called Sharbel and became a priest. Father Sharbel was happy to show his love for God with prayer, penance, and hard work. When he was elderly, Father Sharbel became ill while celebrating Mass. He went home to God on Christmas Eve, 1898. Saint Sharbel is greatly loved in Lebanon and around the world.

Saint Sharbel lived from 1828–1898.

He lived his whole life in Lebanon.

We celebrate his feast day on July 24.

Saint Sharbel, please teach me how to talk to God daily in prayer.

Saint Elizabeth Seton

When Elizabeth's husband died, she needed money to take care of her five children. So she got a job as a teacher. This helped solve her problem.

Elizabeth was a very good teacher. Soon a priest asked her to begin a school for girls. The school was in Maryland. It became the first Catholic school in the United States!

Elizabeth loved God very much. She started a new group of teaching sisters called the Sisters of Charity. By the time Elizabeth died, more Catholic schools were opening all over America.

Saint Elizabeth will help us when we have problems to solve.

Saint Elizabeth lived from 1774–1821.

She was born in the United States.

We celebrate her feast day on January 4.

Blessed Junipero Serra

As a young Franciscan priest, Junipero wanted to be a missionary. In 1749, his superiors asked for volunteers to go to North America. Father Junipero rejoiced. He sailed to Mexico. After several years, he and his fellow missionaries traveled to California. They brought the love of Jesus to the native people there. The people learned to love and trust them. Father Junipero built nine missions. Over the years, nearly six thousand people were baptized. Father Junipero loved and protected the native people.

Blessed Junipero lived from 1713–1784.

He was born in Spain.

We celebrate his feast day on July 1.

Blessed Junipero, please show me how to be unselfish.

Saint Thecla

Thecla was young and beautiful. She wanted to learn about the true God. One day Saint Paul came to her town. There he taught about Jesus. He told Thecla that she could dedicate her life to Jesus. But Thecla's family believed in pagan gods, and they were angry. Thecla was taken to court and sentenced to death. She was brave and faithful. She prayed to Jesus to protect her. He did protect her! Finally, Thecla was set free. She spent the rest of her life praying and teaching about the love of Jesus.

Saint Thecla lived in the first century A.D.

She was born in Asia Minor (now Turkey).

We celebrate her feast day on September 23.

Saint Thecla, please show me how to love Jesus bravely as you did.

Saint Patrick

When Patrick was sixteen, kidnappers brought him to Ireland. There he took care of sheep for a cruel man. He escaped after six years.

Patrick went to Britain. He became a priest. Soon he was made Bishop of Ireland. It was hard for him to go back to Ireland, but he did! At that time the Irish people did not worship God. Patrick taught them to love God and his Son, Jesus. He helped them to love one another. Patrick built churches. He helped men become priests and women become nuns.

Saint Patrick will help us teach our friends who need to learn about Jesus.

Saint Patrick lived from about 387–493.

He may have been born in Scotland.

We celebrate his feast day on March 17.

Saint Brigid
of Ireland

Brigid's parents were baptized by Saint Patrick himself. As a child, Brigid was kind and good. One day she gave a pail of milk to a poor family. She prayed that her mother would not be upset. When she got home, her pail was full again! Brigid wanted to follow Jesus. She had seven good friends. With them, she started the first convent in Ireland. Soon the convent became a center for religion and art. She started other convents, too. Brigid died many years later. She was buried near Saint Patrick.

Saint Brigid lived from around 450–525.

She was born in Ireland.

We celebrate her feast day on February 1.

Saint Brigid, help me to spread Jesus's love as you did.

Blessed Miguel Pro

Miguel wanted to be a priest. But there was trouble in Mexico. The leaders didn't want anyone to be Catholic. Miguel had to leave. Finally he became a priest in Belgium. Then Father Miguel went home to Mexico. He disguised himself. Sometimes he dressed as a beggar or a street cleaner. He said Mass in secret. He brought Holy Communion into people's homes. Then the police caught him and put him in prison. Mexico's leaders gave the order to shoot him. Father Miguel was very brave. He said, "Long live Christ the King!"

Blessed Miguel, please teach me to be faithful and brave.

Blessed Miguel lived from 1891–1927.

He was born in Mexico.

We celebrate his feast day on November 23.

Saint Agnes

When Saint Agnes was alive, a cruel man ruled Rome. He made it against the law to believe in Jesus. Agnes loved Jesus and believed in him. She would not pray to any false gods.

Agnes was pretty. She knew that God had made her, and she respected her body. Some young men wanted to marry Agnes. But she said "no." One man became angry with her. He had her arrested for being a Christian. The judge decided that Agnes had to die. She was only thirteen years old.

Saint Agnes will help us to know and do what pleases God.

Saint Agnes lived from about 290–304.

She was born in Italy.

We celebrate her feast day on January 21.

Saint Stanislaus Kostka

Stanislaus was born to an important Polish family. He and Paul, his older brother, received a good education in Vienna, Austria. Although Paul laughed at him, Stanislaus decided to join the Jesuit order. He traveled to Rome and became a novice. He prayed and studied hard. After ten months, his health failed, and he died.

Saint Stanislaus lived from 1550–1568.

He was born in Poland.

His feast day is August 15.

His brother was very sorry for treating Stanislaus badly. Eventually, Paul became a Jesuit priest. He was present when his younger brother was declared a blessed. Now Stanislaus is a saint!

Saint Stanislaus, please give me your courage to be true to Jesus.

Saint Frances Xavier Cabrini

Frances was a teacher in Italy. The bishop asked her to begin a new religious congregation. She founded the Missionary Sisters of the Sacred Heart of Jesus. One day Mother Cabrini met with Pope Leo XIII. She asked to go to China as a missionary. Instead, the Pope sent her to help Italian immigrants in the United States. She and her sisters started schools, hospitals, and children's homes. In 1946, Mother Cabrini became the first United States citizen to be declared a saint.

Saint Frances, please teach me to love and respect everyone I meet.

Saint Frances lived from 1850–1917.

She was born in Italy.

We celebrate her feast day on November 13.

Saint Maximilian Kolbe

When Raymond was twelve, he saw the Blessed Mother. After that, he tried to be more obedient. Raymond became a priest when he grew up. He was called Father Maximilian. He started a prayer group to honor Mary. He also printed magazines about Jesus and Mary.

Saint Maximilian lived from 1894–1941.

He was born in Poland.

We celebrate his feast day on August 14.

Soldiers captured Father Maximilian during World War II. They were going to kill a prisoner who had a wife and children. Father Maximilian wanted to save him. He told the soldiers, "Stop! Take me instead." And that is what they did.

Saint Maximilian will help us when we need to be brave.

Saint Margaret of Scotland

Margaret married King Malcolm of Scotland. Queen Margaret wanted to help her new people. She made visits to the poor and to prisoners every day. Together Malcolm and Margaret built churches and monasteries. One day, King Malcolm and his son Edward rode off to defend Scotland from enemy raiders. They were killed in battle. Queen Margaret was very sad. She prayed for her dear husband and son. She herself died just a few days later.

Saint Margaret lived from 1045–1093.

She was born in England.

We celebrate her feast day on November 16.

Saint Margaret, please show me how to be a loving member of my family.

Saint Moses the Black

Moses was a slave in Egypt. He was also a thief. One day he joined a gang of bandits. Soon Moses became their leader. Moses's enemies were looking for him. He hid with some monks in the desert of Scete. The monks prayed often. They were very kind to Moses. Moses was finally sorry for his crimes. He decided to learn about the monks' faith. He asked to be baptized. He became a monk and then a priest. Father Moses wanted to help all people to live in peace.

Saint Moses, please give me your courage to choose what is right.

Saint Moses lived from 330–405.

He was born in Egypt.

We celebrate his feast day on August 28.

Saint Monica

Monica and her husband had two sons and one daughter. Augustine, the oldest boy, was always in trouble.

After his father died, Augustine still caused problems. He would not study. He followed false gods. But Monica would not give up on him. For seventeen years she asked God to help her son. Finally, Augustine changed. He was baptized. He began to write and teach about Jesus. Augustine became one of our Church's greatest saints!

Saint Monica lived from 333–387.

She was born in North Africa (now the country of Algiers).

We celebrate her feast day on August 27.

Are you praying for something or someone? Don't give up! Saint Monica teaches us that God always hears our prayers and does what is best for us.

Saint Paul Miki

When he was young, Paul went to a Catholic school. He learned to teach about Jesus. He wanted everyone to find the joy of being Christian. Many people listened to him. The emperor of Japan believed lies about Christians. He tried to send them all away. Paul and other Christians hid. They taught about Jesus anyway. Twenty-six brave Christians were captured and put to death. They loved Jesus with all their hearts. Paul Miki was one of them. In just one year, he would have become a priest.

Saint Paul Miki, please help me to follow Jesus's teachings the way you did.

Saint Paul lived from around 1562–1597.

He was born in Japan.

We celebrate his feast day on February 6.

Saint Teresa of the Andes

Juanita was a happy girl in Santiago, Chile. On the day of her first Communion, something wonderful happened. Jesus actually spoke to her! This changed her life. She began to pray more and to go to daily Mass. Juanita read about Saint Thérèse of Lisieux, the famous French Carmelite nun. Eventually, Juanita decided to enter the Carmelite Monastery of the Holy Spirit in Los Andes. She took the name Sister Teresa. When she was 20, she became very ill. Before she died, she made her religious vows.

Saint Teresa lived from 1900–1920.

She was born in Chile.

We celebrate her feast day on April 12.

Saint Teresa of the Andes, please teach me how to give my whole life to Jesus.

Saint Martin de Porres

Martin's mother had once been a slave. His father was a Spanish nobleman. Sometimes people were unkind to Martin because he had dark skin like his mother. But Martin loved everyone. When he was twelve, he learned how to take care of sick people and animals. He took care of the poorest people, especially the African slaves.

Saint Martin lived from 1579–1639.

He was born in Peru.

We celebrate his feast day on November 3.

Martin joined the followers of Saint Dominic. The priests wanted him to become a priest. But Martin wanted to serve God and others as a brother.

We can ask Saint Martin to help us love all people just as God loves all of us!

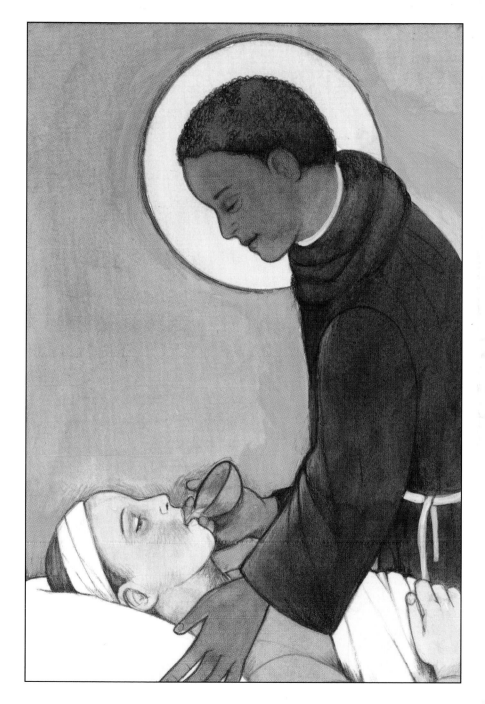

Saint Bridget of Sweden

Bridget and her husband, Ulf, loved each other and their eight children. They prayed every day. Bridget especially honored Jesus, who suffered and died for us all. "How much you love us, Jesus," she whispered. "Thank you for loving us so much!" After Ulf died and their children grew up, Bridget started a new order of sisters, the Brigittines. They spent their lives praying, sacrificing, and working for others. Bridget finally traveled to the Holy Land. At the shrines there, she had many visions of Jesus.

Saint Bridget lived from 1303–1373.

She was born in Sweden.

We celebrate her feast day on July 23.

Saint Bridget, please remind me to thank Jesus often for his sacrifice for us.

Saint Benedict the Moor

Benedict's parents were Ethiopian slaves who became Christians in Sicily. Their son, Benedict, was granted his freedom. He worked hard to support his parents and himself. One day, some boys were throwing rocks at him. Brother Jerome, a Franciscan friar, defended Benedict. After that, Benedict was invited to join the Franciscans. In time, he became the leader of his community. Benedict never learned to read or write, but he was wise and fair. He was loved by all around him.

Saint Benedict, please teach me how to be calm and patient.

Saint Benedict the Moor lived from 1524–1589.

He spent his whole life in Italy.

We celebrate his feast day on April 4.

Saint Joan of Arc

Saint Joan never learned to read or write. But she knew how to pray! When Joan was thirteen, she heard an angel's voice. "You will help France win the war against England," the angel said. *I can't do that!* Joan thought. But when she was sixteen, Joan *did* lead the French army into battle. And they won! Then the English leaders arrested her. They put her in jail. They said she was a witch. When Joan said she was only obeying God, she was put to death.

Saint Joan of Arc lived from 1412–1431.

She was born in France.

We celebrate her feast day on May 30.

Saint Joan will help us to be brave and strong and always tell the truth.

Saint Alberto Hurtado Cruchaga

The poor children in Chile loved Father Alberto. They ran to him when his old green truck came down the street. Father always had a smile for each one. He built a large home for poor and homeless children. He called it Christ's House. He started schools and shelters, too. He helped people find jobs. Father Alberto believed all people should help each other. Pope Benedict XVI named him a saint in 2005.

Saint Alberto, help me to be cheerful, kind, and loving just like you.

Saint Alberto lived from 1901–1952.

He was born in Chile.

We celebrate his feast day on August 18.

Saint Edith Stein

Edith was born into a loving Jewish family. As a teenager, she didn't believe in God. One day, she read a book by Saint Teresa of Avila. After that, Edith decided to follow Jesus. She was baptized a Catholic and became a Carmelite nun. Her religious name was Sister Teresa Benedicta of the Cross. During World War II, the Nazis imprisoned and killed millions of Jews and other innocent people.

Saint Edith Stein lived from 1891–1942.

She was born in Germany.

We celebrate her feast day on August 9.

Sister Teresa was sent to a prison camp because of her Jewish family. Sister Teresa died praying for the Jewish people who were suffering so much.

Saint Edith Stein, please give me your courage.

Saint Nicholas

Nicholas's parents were rich. But Nicholas loved poor people. When he grew up he became a bishop, and his love for God and the poor was even stronger. The people loved him, too. They told stories about his kindness. One story was about a poor man. He needed money so that his daughter could get married. Nicholas solved the problem. He threw a bag of gold down the man's chimney!

Saint Nicholas lived from about 280–342.

He was born in Asia Minor (now part of the country of Turkey).

We celebrate his feast day on December 6.

Today, some children call Saint Nicholas "Santa Claus." He teaches us to love and to give.

Whenever we feel selfish, we can ask Saint Nicholas to help us to share.

Saint Germaine

Germaine loved Jesus with all her heart. She took care of the family sheep. Her stepmother was unkind to her. Her parents wouldn't allow her to go to school. They made her live in the barn with the sheep. Germaine never complained. She taught the neighborhood children how to love Jesus. They loved Germaine, too. Germaine went to Mass every morning. The sheep never wandered while she was gone! Her parents finally were sorry for the way they had treated her. Germaine forgave them. She was just twenty-two when she died.

Saint Germaine, help me to be patient and forgiving.

Saint Germaine lived from 1579–1601.

She lived her whole life in France.

We celebrate her feast day on June 15.

Saint Peter Claver

Peter lived in Spain. When he was twenty-two, he became a Jesuit priest. His friend Brother Alphonsus told him about some Africans. Many were being kidnapped. Slave ships took them far away to the New World. Father Peter had to help them! He sailed to Colombia. There he found many frightened, sick Africans. Father Peter served the enslaved people for forty years. He believed that everyone should be treated kindly and with justice. Father Peter baptized many of the Africans. He taught them to love Jesus.

Saint Peter lived from 1580–1654.

He was born in Spain.

We celebrate his feast day on September 9.

Saint Peter, you helped many suffering people. Teach me to be kind to everyone, too.

Saint Catherine of Siena

Catherine had twenty-five brothers and sisters! She loved them and she loved God. Her parents wanted her to get married. But Catherine wanted to give her life to God. When she was sixteen, she gave her heart to God.

Saint Catherine lived from 1347–1380.

She was born in Italy.

We celebrate her feast day on April 29.

Catherine took care of sick people and prisoners. She also prayed and worked for peace. She begged the leaders of the Church and of the world to stop fighting. Even the Pope listened to her!

People loved this happy "servant of God." She helped bring peace back to God's Church.

If we ask her, Saint Catherine will help us always to be peacemakers.

Saint Pedro de San José Betancur

Twenty-three-year-old Pedro wanted to bring the Gospel message to the New World. He traveled by ship to Cuba, then to Honduras, and on to Guatemala. When he arrived there, the Franciscan brothers helped him. He became a Third Order Franciscan. Brother Pedro operated a hospital, a homeless shelter, and a school for poor children. He started a religious congregation, too. He was just forty-one when he died. Saint Pedro is the first Guatemalan to be named a saint.

Saint Pedro lived from 1626–1667.

He was born in the Canary Islands.

We celebrate his feast day on April 25.

Saint Pedro, please help me to become as unselfish as you were.

Saint Marguérite d'Youville

Marguérite married a man named François. When he died, he left large debts. Marguérite worked hard to pay them off. She also wanted to help the poor around her. Some young women asked to join Marguérite. They began the Sisters of Charity. Because of the color of their habits, the sisters were also called the Grey Nuns. The sisters operated a hospital in Montréal. Today the Grey Nuns still work throughout Canada, the United States, and in other countries. Saint Marguérite is the first native-born Canadian saint.

Saint Marguérite, please teach me to be caring.

Saint Marguérite lived from 1701–1771.

She was born in Québec.

Her feast day is October 16.

What Is a Blessed?

A person is called a blessed when the Pope declares that he or she has lived a holy life and is now in heaven. Usually a miracle has taken place through prayers to the person. This is the next-to-last step on the road to being officially declared a saint.

What Is a Saint?

A person is called a saint when the Pope declares that the holy person can be honored and imitated by the whole Church. Usually a second miracle has been proven. This is the final step in being officially declared a saint.

What Is a Miracle?

A miracle is an amazing event that can't be explained by the usual laws of nature. The greatest miracle of all occurred when Jesus rose from the dead. When saints or blesseds perform miracles, God is working those miracles through them.